This book is dedicated to:
the snuggles
and nightmares
and mommies and daddies
and wasp stings
and silliness of everyday life.

© 2016 Dan the Fish

A Child's Voice: Volume One

ISBN #978-0-9965956-4-3

Contact us at:

DantheFish9@gmail.com

Snugglepoems

By Fionn Coppoc

Illustrated by Sara Merritt

Jump

jump up and down

your hands fall down on the floor

your hair wiggles

your body moves

jumping is like flying and falling

my heart giggles

I can't get up

Silly

I am silly.

My dad is silly.

My mom is silly.

My brother is silly.

Silly sticks out its tongue

Silly jumps rope

Silly goes blah blah blah

Sometimes, Silly breaks its leg.

When I feel silly, I roll around on the ceiling

When I feel silly, I smash my Dad and my dog barks at me

When I'm done being silly, I fall down.

And nothing happens.

Ophelia

fun Ophelia
home run Ophelia
recess in the sun Ophelia

race Ophelia
home base Ophelia
tie her shoelace Ophelia

weekend Ophelia
my friend Ophelia
birthday invite send
Ophelia

I play with Ophelia
every day with Ophelia
after school

Humming

My humming is happy
it makes me feel good
My humming is soft
it makes my body proud

My brother doesn't like it when I hum

He says please stop humming
I'm not trying to do anything
to make you be distracted and annoyed

but humming makes me happy
I usually hum every day

I can't stop

when I start
I can't stop

The Rainy Day

Once upon a time
it was a shiny day outside
and I was a TV, and I could walk
and see

One day, it was just dark and rainy
and the trampoline was blown up
and broken apart into tiny pieces

The dragon blew the whole world up
and lived in outer space

I put the world back together again
but in a different way
so all the people who were friends
lived together, and on the same street

it was awesome

They always took a walk all together
unless it was raining or snowing,
when they would go back home
and watch TV or something

The End

Buttheads

Buttheads fart ohs
In their sleep they fart
Buttheads draw with their heads
Buttheads fart ketchup too

If I was a butthead,
I would fart televisions
If you were a butthead,
you would fart kittens

If brother was a butthead,
he would be a sleepy butthead

being a butthead is farting
being a butthead smells like French fries

My Dad
is a butthead

Space

Mars has iron
Saturn has rings
the sun is gas and fire

we live on Earth
we have lots of water
and that's where my brother is

he plays Legos with me
and Star Wars Battlefront

Earth is pretty awesome

What Do You Do With a Fire

If your clothes catch on fire
stop, drop and roll

If your house catches on fire
get out as fast as you can!

If your poop catches on fire
wait, just wait
and see what happens

Screen Time

The wind is my father
and it is whispering
that I should have screen time

My mom is a zebra
and she says
I have to earn
screen time

My brother is a joker
and he says
I should have
screen time
all the time

I am a booger
and I say
I should have
screen time
forever

we are each a piece of god

He is you
He is me
He is crayons
He is pictures
He is statues
He is guitars
He is underwear
He is everything

My Friend Tigress

is a great player at basketball
is a great player at soccer
is a great player at golf
is good at baseball

My friend Tigress is
funny, is
fun, is
playful, is
jumping

My friend Tigress
is walking
is running
is hopping
is rolling

My friend Tigress is
a tiger, is
yellow, is
black, is
wearing clothes

My friend Tigress
is wearing pants

She is my friend.

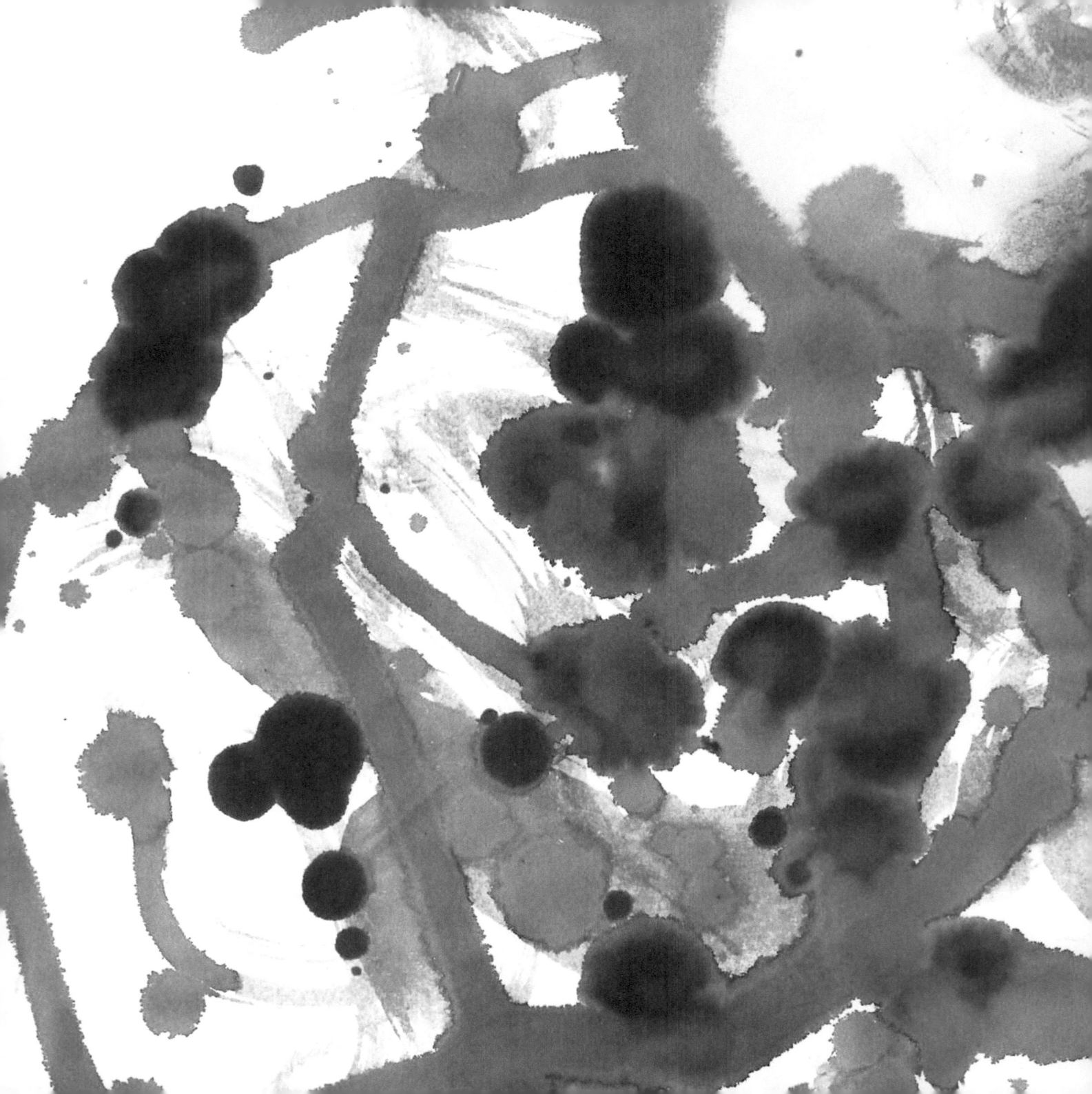

Infinity Mad

because you hurt my feelings
and I thought you were being mean
I got mad
infinity mad

like everyone's being mean
like a dog is growling
like my eyes sort of close
and my heart is gone

I slam the door
I throw stuff
and I cry sometimes

I cry
because I want
what I want

Don't Think

When I don't think, I start thinking

I try to think
I don't stop

I always think
I thought *does thinking make poems harder*
Then my dad says yes
Then I started never thinking
unless I'm at school

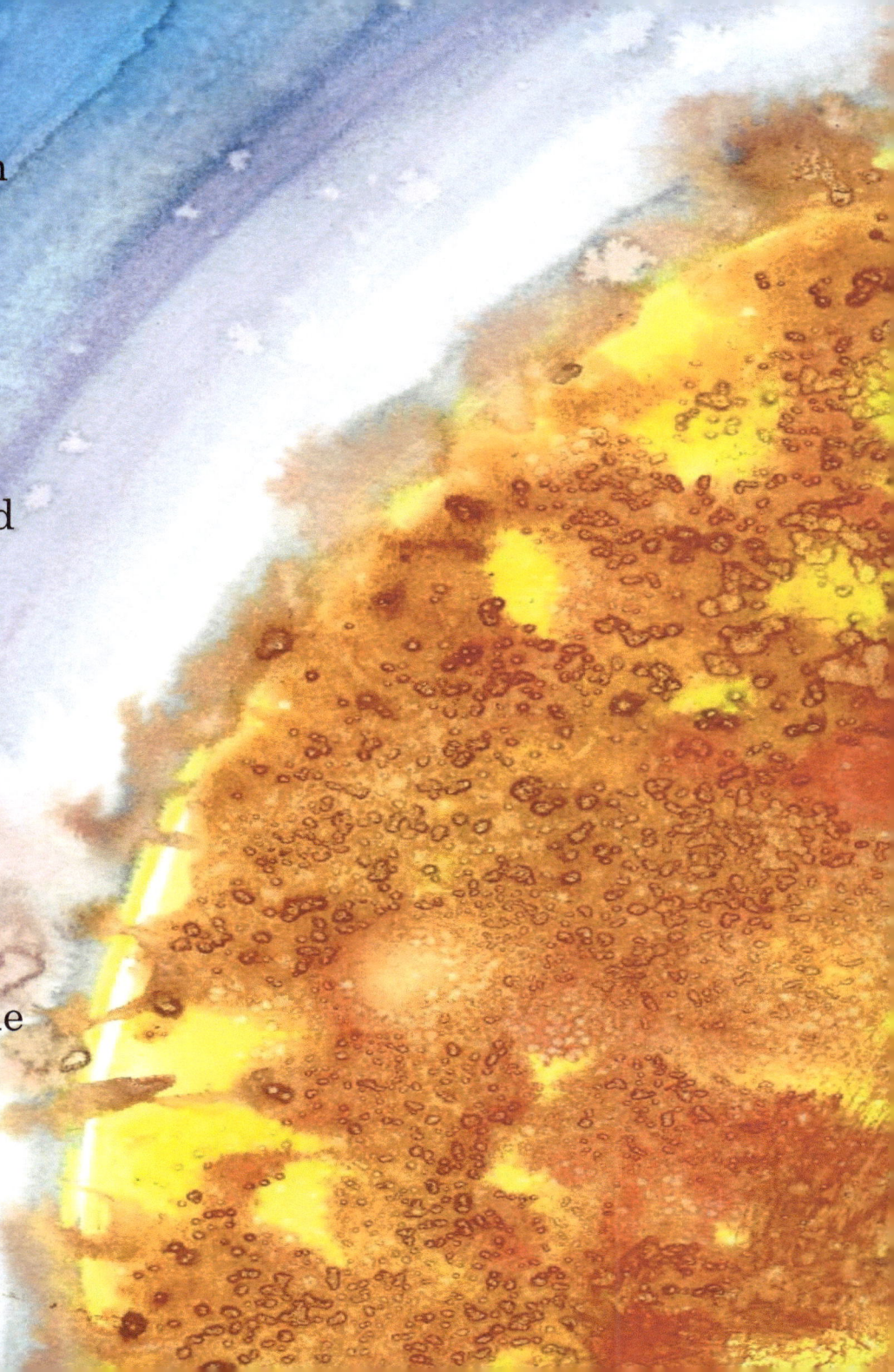

In Space

there is the Sun in
space
and Earth
and Mercury
Jupiter
Mars

there are stars and
the stars are suns

Suns are bright
The sun has fire

I don't remember
why

Space gives us
nighttime when the
sun's shadow is on
us

I don't remember
the rest

Similes for Mommy

I love you like stink loves poo

I love you like lions love running

I love you like dogs love snuggles

fans love blowing

fires love burning

I love you like guitars love songs

because you snuggle like a kitty

because you paint with me

because you're really good at Monopoly

but I usually always win

I love you for your music

and your singing

and your love

like something warm

Wasps

I don't want to write
a poem about wasps

I got stung once,
twice

When I think about wasps
My body worries

My stomach rumbles

I wish none of that would happen

I wish I could think about dreams

My dreams help a lot

Except my brain just goes thump
right back to the wasps

and I can't sleep anymore

The Nightmare

I had a nightmare last night
it was about a big giant ant

it had sharp legs

it sat on my arm
then disappeared

Nightmares are scary

When I get scared, I cry

I call my Mom

and she comes to me

and talks to me

she tells me to go on her bed

and I feel like the
nightmare follows me

being with Mommy helps

but I still feel like it's
following me

I might see it again tonight

I don't know how to get
better

For Mommy

I love you
I wanna hug you
I wanna kiss you
Let's play games
like Hoot Owl Hoot
Let's help put away
the dishwasher

I feel you in my shoulders
bumping me
squishy
I really want to hug you

I love you
Fionn

Moses

loves to snuggle

Moses

hugs and kisses

Moses

likes long naps

treats

and two syllable words

Moses

wants to write poems

but he can't

because they are my poems

and dogs can't write

Protests by Fionn and *his dad, Jim*

I don't like pipelines because they break
and when they break, oil hits the water
and some rivers go to different states
they give the states water

I went to a protest, and the police
were making a bad choice
because they listened to the person
who wanted the pipeline
and they arrested the people
who blocked the pipeline trucks

I felt scared

I tell him the officers are scared too
but they have a job to do

and my son, Fionn Preston Coppoc, 6 years old
has learned injustice
before long division

in protests
in some of the protests
the police officers
even treat people bad

they should not arrest people
and treat them bad

they should arrest the pipeline people
for trying to make the pipeline
because it could break under the river
and people could die

*Fionn's mother is a water protector
we speak of attack dogs and riot police
of the possibility of tear gas on the wind*

the next protest, Fionn stays home

I made posters of protests
They said "circle of love"
and "we don't want death; we want love"

I made them so I could
have a protest
even if I couldn't go to the
real protest
so our house could protest

Someday I will make
posters about how to stop
the pipeline

Today I made posters
about love

you know in some movies
when people don't have
love
their hearts are gone?

Protests are about love
because if you don't have
love
maybe you are lonely

and if you're lonely,
maybe you are scared

and if you are scared
you might not speak

About the Author

Fionn Preston Coppoc is a first grader at Kate Mitchell Elementary in Ames, Iowa, with a full life of family, soccer, pets, singing, Legos, friends, hiking, swimming, reading, silly jokes and as many cartoons and video games as he can get away with. His poetry life began as a simple birthday present for his mother, and has expanded into slams and jams and open mics and public readings and now this book. Other current projects include drawing comics for family, and teaching his dog Moses how to shake hands.

About the Illustrator

In addition to her full-time role as Education Manager for Reiman Gardens at Iowa State University, Sara Merritt is an Ames, Iowa artist passionate about informal education- hands-on learning that happens anywhere and everywhere.

With 20 years of experience teaching everything from photography, drawing and painting, to martial arts and belly dance, Sara loves to learn new things. She currently performs with the Mirage Middle Eastern Dance Troupe, and serves as President of the Ames Community Arts Council. Sara has a Bachelor of Arts in Art, Sexuality, & Aesthetic Perception from the University of Massachusetts-Amherst, as well as a Master of Fine Arts degree from the San Francisco Art Institute, and believes absolutely that everyone can be an artist.

www.ingramcontent.com/pod-product-compliance
Lightning Source LLC
Chambersburg PA
CBHW042117040426
42449CB00002B/78